The Lord is my Shepherd

THE TWENTY~THIRD PSALM

The Lord is my Shepherd

THE TWENTY~THIRD PSALM

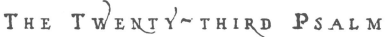

illustrated by GENNADY SPIRIN

PHILOMEL BOOKS

P A T R I C I A   L E E   G A U C H ,   E D I T O R

PHILOMEL BOOKS
A division of Penguin Young Readers Group.
Published by The Penguin Group.
Penguin Group (USA) Inc., 375 Hudson Street, New York, NY 10014, U.S.A.
Penguin Group (Canada), 90 Eglinton Avenue East, Suite 700, Toronto, Ontario M4P 2Y3, Canada
(a division of Pearson Penguin Canada Inc.).
Penguin Books Ltd, 80 Strand, London WC2R 0RL, England.
Penguin Ireland, 25 St. Stephen's Green, Dublin 2, Ireland (a division of Penguin Books Ltd.).
Penguin Group (Australia), 250 Camberwell Road, Camberwell, Victoria 3124, Australia (a division
of Pearson Australia Group Pty Ltd).
Penguin Books India Pvt Ltd, 11 Community Centre, Panchsheel Park, New Delhi – 110 017, India.
Penguin Group (NZ), 67 Apollo Drive, Rosedale, North Shore 0745, Auckland, New Zealand
(a division of Pearson New Zealand Ltd.)
Penguin Books (South Africa) (Pty) Ltd, 24 Sturdee Avenue, Rosebank, Johannesburg 2196,
South Africa.
Penguin Books Ltd, Registered Offices: 80 Strand, London WC2R 0RL, England.

Published simultaneously in Canada.
Manufactured in China by South China Printing Co. Ltd.
Design by Semadar Megged.   The illustrations are rendered in oil paint on canvas.
Library of Congress Cataloging–in–Publication Data
Bible. O.T. Psalms XXIII. English. Authorized. 2008.
The Lord is my shepherd / [illustrated by] Gennady Spirin.   p. cm.
1. Bible. O.T. Psalms XXIII—Juvenile literature. I. Spirin, Gennadii. II. Title.
BS145023rd 2008   223'.2052034—dc22   2007020394
ISBN 978–0–399–24527–5
10 9 8 7 6 5 4 3 2 1

To Mitropolitan Laurus

The LORD is my shepherd;

I shall not want.

He maketh me to lie down
in green pastures:

he leadeth me
beside the still waters.

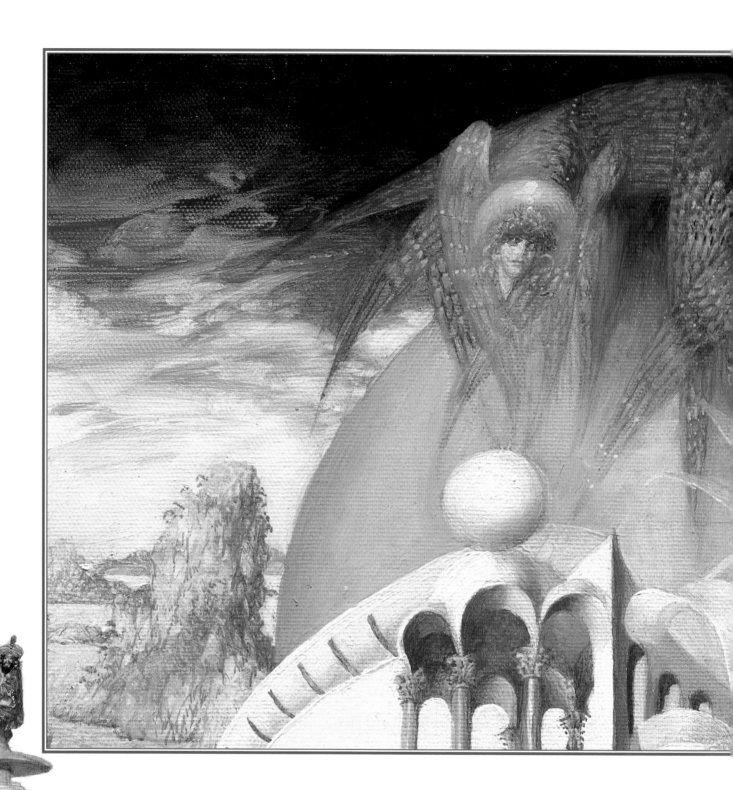

He restoreth my soul:
he leadeth me in the paths

of righteousness
for his name's sake.

Yea, though I walk
through the valley
of the shadow
of death,

I will fear no evil:
for thou art with me;

thy rod and thy staff
they comfort me.

Thou preparest a table before me

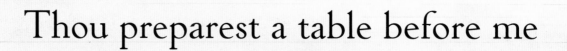

in the presence of mine enemies:

thou anointest
my head with oil;
my cup runneth over.

Surely goodness and mercy shall

follow me all the days of my life:

and I will dwell in the house

of the LORD for ever.

The LORD is my shepherd; I shall not want.

He maketh me to lie down in green pastures: he leadeth me beside the still waters.

He restoreth my soul: he leadeth me in the paths of righteousness for his name's sake.

Yea, though I walk through the valley of the shadow of death, I will fear no evil: for thou art with me; thy rod and thy staff they comfort me.

Thou preparest a table before me in the presence of mine enemies: thou anointest my head with oil; my cup runneth over.

Surely goodness and mercy shall follow me all the days of my life: and I will dwell in the house of the LORD for ever.